LEAD LIKE A COACH

By Michael Duke

DISCLAIMER

This book details the author's personal experiences with and opinions about leadership. The author is not a licensed attorney or financial professional.

The author and publisher are providing this book and its contents on an "as is" basis and make no representations or warranties of any kind with respect to this book or its contents. The author and publisher disclaim all such representations and warranties, including for example warranties of merchantability and consulting advice for a particular purpose. In addition, the author and publisher do not represent or warrant that the information accessible via this book is accurate, complete or current.

The statements made about products and services have not been evaluated by the U.S. government. Please consult with your own legal or accounting professional regarding the suggestions and recommendations made in this book.

Except as specifically stated in this book, neither the author or publisher, nor any authors, contributors, or other representatives will be liable for damages arising out of or in connection with the use of this book. This is a comprehensive limitation of liability that applies to all damages of any kind, including (without limitation) compensatory; direct, indirect or consequential damages; loss of data, income or profit; loss of or damage to property and claims of third parties.

You understand that this book is not intended as a substitute for consultation with a licensed legal or accounting professional. Before you begin any change your lifestyle in any way, you will consult a licensed professional to ensure that you are doing what's best for your situation.

This book provides content related to leadership topics. As such, use of this book implies your acceptance of this disclaimer.

To Coach John Wooden.

You have inspired me and countless others to lead from the deep well of our values.

Thank you!

I firmly believe that you can change the world by changing the people who matter to you. You influence people and change them by caring about them, by involving yourself with them, and by interacting with them in their lives.
-- Michael Duke

TABLE OF CONTENTS

LEAD LIKE A COACH: INTRODUCTION

I firmly believe that you can change the world by changing the people who matter to you. You influence people and change them by caring about them, by involving yourself with them, and by interacting with them in their lives. Ignoring people doesn't help them to become better, and criticism alone doesn't do it either. If you want people to get better, you have to care about them.

Leadership is the greatest job in the world. To influence lives and interact with people in a way that makes them better is the essence of coaching. Too many times, we get into ruts as managers. We come to believe that effective management is just a matter of creating a list of tasks and checking them off as "done." Sometimes, we think if we can take this piece of paper and put it over there, our job is done. But in my opinion, you haven't even begun to do your job unless you've influenced the people on your team for their good.

I believe that if you look at your responsibilities, you will discover that you are a leader. You have taken on the responsibility of leadership. If you look at your role through the lens of a coach, however, you will lead differently. So, how do coaches lead differently than managers, bosses, and supervisors? If we showed up to work every single day and led like coaches, what would be different?

Making shots counts, but not as much
as the people who make them.
-- Mike Krzyzewski

It's About the People, Not the Numbers

I'll share a thought with you from a great coach by the name of Albert Einstein. He said the things that really count in life can't necessarily be counted. If you're focused solely on numbers in your job right now, I will dare to say that you're missing the point because what's truly important in life cannot be defined by numbers.

Now, I can almost hear you out there asking, "But, Michael, aren't revenues important? Isn't market share important? Aren't profits and the number of units sold important?" Of course, numbers are important. I'm not saying they aren't, and neither was Einstein. But coaches understand that you don't achieve victory with a direct attack. Coaches know that you focus on the people, and that requires an indirect attack. In other words, concentrate on the people, and the numbers will come.

We have all heard, read, and seen coaches who were all about the win, all about the "W." We also know that many sports programs have gotten into trouble as a result. The truth is that coaches who focus just on the score may be successful short-term, but they're never successful long-term. So, if a coach doesn't focus on the outcome or the score, what does he or she concentrate on?

Do you know the coach who won the most championships in NCAA history? The late and legendary John Wooden. His UCLA Bruins won seven championships in a row and ten in twelve years. If you're a sports fan, you know how great it is when your team wins just one championship. To win twice feels amazing. Three times? Imagine it. Now, try to fathom winning seven in a row! That's what Coach Wooden did.

Coach Wooden also wrote a book called *Wooden on Leadership.* At the end of every chapter is a letter from one of the players about his personal experience at UCLA. One of them said something that really stood out to me. He said: "You know what? Coach Wooden never spoke of winning." Think about that. He never discussed winning; it was never the goal.

So, how does the coach who has won more championships than any other coach win so much without focusing on winning? Does that make any sense to you? Well, if you really stop to think about it, it makes perfect sense. Coach Wooden knew that if you make your people great, they will step up and be great. Then, when greatness is required, you'll win more than you'll lose.

If you read the books by famous coaches like Wooden or Rick Pitino, they will most often say that the team they're most proud of is not one of their championship teams. In Wooden's case, it was the team that went 16-16. When asked about all of his championship teams, he says that they're great players, but the team that went 16-16 were overachievers. He said that they gave him more heart and passion and did more with their talent than any of his championship teams. So, you see, it truly isn't about the numbers.

I'm sure you have plenty of reports to fill out and look at on a regular basis. Are you graded and measured based on a certain metric? Of course you are! And there's nothing wrong with that. It's as it should be. But if you want those numbers to get better, don't focus on the numbers. This is something that's so obvious to a coach. The coach sees the five players on the court, the nine players on the field, or the eleven guys out there working for him, and he thinks to himself: "If I'm going to win the game, I have to make these players great." So, he focuses on the fundamentals of making each player great by building their attitudes, their character, and their performance skills. The coach realizes that the score will take care of itself if he works to make each and every player on the team better.

Building attitude, character, and skill requires a compassionate and caring coach. A lot of people become uncomfortable when you talk about love, but in the book *Love is the Killer App* by Tim Sanders, the author openly uses the word "love" with his colleagues and clients. Of course, as a leader, you don't have to use the word "love" if you don't want to. You can use the words "care" and "concern." But if your people know how

LEAD LIKE A COACH

much you care, is that going to make a difference? Of course it will. Remember that it isn't about you and it isn't about the numbers. It's about your people and making them great. It's about making them great because you care about them first and foremost.

5

One Step at a Time

Sometimes, coaches are hired to turn a team around, and there may be a lot of pressure. The team may not have a good history and hasn't done well in the past. How in the world can a coach turn them around and make them better? Well, it takes time, of course. Author Ken Blanchard calls it the law of 1%. What if the coach could make his or her people 1% better this week? Just 1%. Then, what if they could be 1% better the next week? In 52 weeks, they're 52% better. The way you make people better is just a step at a time.

Here's an example. Coaches redefine what it means to win, and I believe this strategy fits well in the business world. If you create a culture where your team members' relationships with you and with one another are positive and fulfilling, your people will go home every day feeling like winners. In that kind of culture, people give their best, regardless of the final score.

You've probably heard of Coach Vince Lombardi. He was one of the great coaches of his era. In 1958, the Green Bay

Packers didn't have a great year. They only won a single game. The next year, however, they brought in Vince Lombardi, and he led them to a 7-5 season. In his second year as Head Coach the Packers played for the NFL championship. They didn't win it, but he took a team that had had a horrible year and led them to play in the championship in two short years. How does a coach do that? These days, you trade in the off-season, you have free agency, you can even get rid of half of your players and bring in new players if you have the money. Back in Lombardi's day, though, you couldn't do all that. It was very rare to have any substantial trades, so you had to play, in large part; with the hand you were dealt.

In his third year as coach of the Packers, they not only made it to the championship again, they won! In his fourth and fifth years, they won the championship again—three championships in a row To this day; no other team has accomplished this in professional football. In a mere three years, Lombardi changed everything.

It's a pretty dramatic thing to turn around a group that had been performing so poorly, isn't it? But this is what coaches do. They understand it's their job to make a difference. Unfortunately, I don't see this strategy in business very much. But the truth is that your job as a leader is also to make a difference.

It's a great honor to be given a team of people and work to build them up and make them better. It's a great accomplishment to make a difference in the lives of your team. After all, if you don't who will?

Who You Are Matters

In my seminars, I always do an exercise with the participants where we think of qualities that we would not want to see in a coach or leader. The negative answers I get are often things like "demeaning," "dictator," "unapproachable," "distracted," and "self-promoting." When you look at qualities like this that a coach or a leader might exhibit, it's easy to see why business ventures fail, isn't it? When great failures in business are studied, we should conclude that it's people who fail. Businesses don't fail, and teams don't fail. They're only as good as the people who lead them. So, who you are as a leader matters. The kind of person you are matters, and your values matter.

It's much too easy to finally get that title and corner office and forget why you're there. But the greatest leaders are actually servants. The greatest leaders understand that it isn't about them; it's about everybody *but* them—the clients, the employees, and their colleagues.

The measure of who we are is what we do with what we have.
-- Vince Lombardi

Let's think about these qualities in practice. If you've read *The One-Minute Manager* by Ken Blanchard and Spencer Johnson, then you know that the most important minutes you spend every day are the ones you invest in your people. If you go to work every day and invest your time and your energy in your people—your players, so to speak—you're going to be a great leader and a winner. If you're demeaning, distracted, or self-promoting, think about the impact those qualities and behaviors will have on your people. How could a coach like this positively influence the performance of his or her players?

Now, I'm not saying that you have to be perfect as a leader. It's more about striving to be better. When you blow it, you say, "I blew it" and learn from your mistake. If you're transparent, vulnerable, and a human being to your people, you'll have a positive influence. If you're critical, disrespectful, and distant, you'll impact them negatively.

The people on your team need a leader, a coach. Who is going to coach them if you don't? They come to work every day, and they have a lot of things to do, right? It's a lot of paperwork and responsibility, and it takes a lot of patience. Do you think that most of them want to grow and learn and get better? You bet they do. So, who's going to help them get there? Who's going to help them learn what excellence means? Who's going to help them learn what hard work means? Who's going to help them learn how great it feels to do excellent work? Take your role seriously, and never underestimate the influence that you have on those who rely on you to lead them.

Do you remember a great coach, leader, or teacher who influenced your life? You'd be surprised how many people never had such a person to affirm them in their lives. So many people were criticized by their parents or family—aunts, uncles, grandparents. Think about how you feel when you're criticized, as compared to how you feel when you're praised. How do you feel when someone does something that says, "I care about you, I'm here to make you better, and I want to invest myself in you"? How do you feel when someone says, "If you do what I ask you to do, you'll be better. If you do what I ask you to do on the job, I'll make sure that you're successful to the extent that you listen to me, to the extent that you work with me and stay on my team"?

People are thirsty for that kind of caring and affirmation. But it's not just empty. It's not just a vain pat on the back for every little thing. It's about really caring enough to truly invest yourself in making your people better.

Honesty and Integrity

What are some of the good qualities that you would want to see in a coach or leader? Honesty might be one of those qualities. Why is honesty important in coaching? Well, without it, you have no trust. What is an organization without trust? You know the importance of trust if you've ever worked for somebody who says, "Yeah, meet me tomorrow at 4:00, and we'll discuss that." Then, when you arrive at 4:00, that person isn't there.

A friend once told me this story about something that happened at her work place: "It's 10:30a.m., and we're all there in the conference room. The meeting was supposed to start at 8:30a.m., and it's glass-walled. So, we can see that our manager is in his office on the phone for two hours, and we're not allowed to leave the conference room until we have our meeting."

Now, I don't know if that looks like honesty to you, but it isn't honesty to me. If you say you'll be somewhere, you had better be there. If you say you want to talk to somebody about something, be there. If there's a certain date for performance evaluations, you shouldn't have to be reminded to show up. If you care about your people and you're devoted to your people, you should be reminding *them*. After all, performance evaluations are about them, aren't they?

Honesty and integrity are absolutely essential. Let me share another story with you from the Wooden book. Wooden said that he never made the first approach on any high school player. Not once did he approach a high school player on his own. He felt that if the UCLA values were powerful and if they resonated with other high school players or coaches, the players would reach out to UCLA and the Wooden program. So many minorities did reach out because they knew that Coach Wooden would be someone who would give them a shot. He was color blind, and he was one of the early coaches to build a mixed team with different minorities. And they became stars. Wooden said, "Talk about your values. Talk about what's important to you because if it's important to the people around you, they will come and find you."

Do you want to know a great recruiting strategy? It's making sure that everyone around you knows what you believe in. Make sure that everybody you know in your neighborhood, in your church, at work, and in the community knows the kind of leader that you are. Then, the people out there who need a job and hear about your values will call you. They will call you because they want to work for someone who has the same values they have. That's how Wooden built a great team. Unless the players who approached his program understood the values of UCLA and resonated with them, there wasn't even a discussion. Who you are matters, and you have to lead from your values—from honesty and integrity.

Passion = Inspiration

Another important quality in a coach or leader is the ability to be inspirational. But how do you inspire people? The coaches who are inspirational all have this quality in common: passion. It's a contagious emotion, isn't it? Passion is powerful; it's raw enthusiasm. When you're passionate, you're going to have passionate people around you.

Vince Lombardi took a team that looked like losers and played like losers and turned them into winners through passion. Do you have people, departments, or teams that are struggling? Ken Blanchard says, "Everyone's a winner; some people are just disguised as losers and the coach understands the difference." When you look beyond the surface to the heart inside of a person, you're not looking at an external measurement. You're seeing their potential.

Have you seen the movie *Rudy*? Rudy was small, he wasn't very skilled, and he really wasn't much of a football player compared to the other guys. But Rudy had heart and passion, and he was inspiring to the people around him. Never forget that everyone on your team is important. Everyone on your team should be a winner in your eyes. They're there, and you must be committed to them whether they're the "best" performer or the "worst" performer. With passion, you'll make every single member of your team great.

Thirteen players on the Green Bay Packers' 1958 losing team went on under Lombardi to become what we call "all pros" today. Out of 22 selected, 13 became first team all-stars. Think about the kind of speech Lombardi must have given them when he took over: "I know that you all think you're losers. Look at the season you've had. They're telling you that you're losers, but I'm telling you that you're not losers. You're winners. Don't look at the scoreboard. I know what's inside of you, and if you'll listen to me, if you'll pay attention to me, and if you'll do what I ask you to do, I will make you great." Think about the power of a coach to make people better, to challenge them to be all that they can be.

Thirteen people on that team answered the call and became better. Thirteen went on to become some of the best of that era.

How did they make that transformation from so much defeat and discouragement to become some of the best players of all time? They needed a coach, and Lombardi had the passion to be an inspirational leader. He believed that every member of his team was a winner, and he inspired them to be better. The players on your team need a coach, too—a coach who cares, a coach who believes they're all winners, a coach who is committed to excellence, and a coach who is passionate and inspirational.

Consistency = Clarity

No matter how inspirational you may try to be, however, your efforts will fall flat if you're inconsistent. When everybody knows the goal, it's something they can rally around. If the goal continues to change, people become frustrated and, understandably, can't get motivated to accomplish the goal. So, to be inspirational, you must be consistent.

In Tony Dungy's book, *Quiet Strength,* he says, "We do what we do—no excuses, no explanations." Tony and his Indianapolis Colts were the winners of Super Bowl XLI in 2007, but he was fired from the Tampa Bay Buccaneers in 2001 because he didn't win fast enough. The very first year after he left the team, the Buccaneers won the Super Bowl. You would think that he would decide, "Maybe something is wrong with the way I'm leading. Maybe something is wrong with the way I direct my team. Maybe I should change." But no, he continued to do what he did—no excuses, no explanations. And it took him a few years, but he went on to win the championship in Indianapolis.

The point to this story is that people need consistency. With consistency, comes clarity. We want our employees to be clear about what's required in their jobs, right? We want clarity in the minds of each team member about their roles and responsibilities. The biggest problem with clarity, however, is that many times we're lacking clarity ourselves. If we don't yet know who we are, if we haven't decided on our own values, and if we haven't yet established our own priorities, we will be very situational in the way that we lead. We may be viewed as moody by our people, and they may not know if we're coming or going. When we lead in this way, an employee is likely to say, "Is it a good day or a bad day to bring up this issue?" Our approachability suffers.

If, on the other hand, we're confident and clear about our values and expectations, we don't lead like Jekyll and Hyde. No one will ask, "Who is he today?" or "Has she changed the agenda yet again?"

I don't know any way to lead, but by example.

-- Don Shula

Great coaches are consistent because they know that who they are matters and that they're always on stage. The words that you say don't matter nearly as much as the example you set, and if you truly, genuinely care from your heart about the people on your team, it will be crystal clear. So, your values and priorities absolutely matter.

The values that you believe in need to be talked about every single day, and they need to line up with your behavior and the tasks you perform every single day. When this is the case, the only result can be excellence. That's the only outcome because people get better when they're centered on great values and great priorities—consistency and clarity.

The Importance of Consequences

If you're not clear on what you believe in and what's important to you, you're going to have a tough time setting high enough expectations to make your team great. In the movie *Remember the Titans,* there's a great scene where the coach tells the players that when they drop the ball or miss a pass, he'll make them run a mile. Now, I'm aware that you probably wouldn't appreciate being asked to run a mile if you miss your numbers or don't do something right. Your people will do better, however, if they're clear about your expectations and the consequences of not meeting those expectations.

That doesn't mean that you make your people run a mile, of course, but they must know what will happen if they don't apply themselves. If you're a parent, you already understand the power of consequences. Let's say it's 5:00, and you tell your children to clean their rooms before dinner. They drop their video games and go straight to their rooms, cleaning them with excellence and passion, right?

A coach is someone who can give correction
without causing resentment.
-- John Wooden

More likely—if you're like my wife and I (who have five children between the two of us)—your request will get an answer like, "As soon as this video game is done, I'll be happy to go in there" or "I haven't died yet; as soon as I die, I'll go and I'll clean my room." A few minutes later, you might ask, "Johnny, have you cleaned your room yet?" And the stalling continues.

The message here is that the request isn't enough; the direction isn't enough. It's absolutely essential that the consequences which follow the direction clarify the meaning of your request. For instance, you might say, "I want all of my team members to come to the weekly Tuesday meeting at 10:00 a.m." Only half of your team members show up for the first meeting, and there are no negative consequences. The issue is never discussed.

So, what do you think will happen at the next meeting? Fewer than half will come, and eventually, no one will come to the meeting. You'll end up meeting with yourself, and the reason is that you have failed to create negative consequences for not showing up to the meetings. In truth, you didn't really mean what you said. You said that you wanted everybody at the meeting, but it wasn't important enough for you to do anything about it. Just as children test you by not cleaning their rooms, your team at work will test you. It's just human nature. There's something inside all of us that wonders, "Does he/she really mean it?"

Unless you give your team consequences for not meeting your expectations, they won't really believe you mean it. I love to study human behavior. I think it's fascinating. Why do we do what we do? Most of the people that I coach and consult with own their own businesses or are higher-level executives, and the most common response to human behavior in a leadership role is criticism.

People are generally critical of behavior. I call it "seeing the gap." They've done the job for a while and continue to see what the job *ought* to be. So, they always see what needs to be done better. It's just like when a kid cleans her room, and you say, "Well, you did a pretty good job, but you need to tuck those corners in tighter, dust over here, and organize your closet." Yes, you want your people to be better, but if all you do is criticize, even if it feels like the most natural thing to do, your people will tune you out. Eventually, if all they hear is negativity, they will tune you out completely.

Even with our children, we may want them to be great athletes or great students, but we can't only criticize them. If we want the people around us in our departments to become great, we can't just tell them all of the stuff that they still need to do better.

Don't Ignore Your People

Another bad habit of many leaders is to ignore behavior. We're busy—too busy to say anything about a good job that someone has done or discuss work that needs to be corrected. We're distracted, we have big things to do, and we don't have the time to say "Good job" or "You need to work on that a bit." After all, it's a hassle, right? It's easier just to ignore it. We think to ourselves, "Why do they need someone to tell them over and over and over again? Shouldn't they know what their job is? Shouldn't they know what excellence looks like?"

But think about a coach who takes that attitude. He shows up to practice and says, "You guys know what to do. Just go do it!" There's no leadership there, right? Coaching is about reviewing and revisiting the fundamentals. It's talking about the basics of integrity, the basics of excellence, the basics of hard work, and showing your team through teaching and example what integrity, excellence, and hard work look like. When you do that, people are inspired. When you ignore them, they are defeated.

If you've ever had a kid in Little League or if you were in Little League yourself, imagine sitting in the stands cheering your team on while the coach sits on the sidelines reading the newspaper. Wouldn't you be outraged by a leader who is so detached and uninvolved? So, make sure that you don't ignore your people. They are your greatest assets. If you and your team are going to win and be the best, it will be because you invested yourself in each and every player on your team. There is no way to make your team excellent without spending time with them and without talking to them face-to-face, one-on-one.

We live in a day and age where everyone wants to do everything through e-mails and text messages. I get several e-mail newsletters, and recently, one included an article entitled, "Is it Okay to Terminate People Via E-mail?" It's hard to imagine, but leaders reprimand, criticize, and even terminate people via e-mail. Why? Because they're weenies! They're afraid of the face-to-face, of the confrontation, of the possibility of hurting someone's feelings or making them angry. Even as leaders, they don't want the responsibility that comes with it—which involves sometimes feeling anxious and having to deal with unpleasant situations. Instead, they escape the unpleasantness by handling it via e-mail.

E-mails and text messages have a place, but it's a transactional place to share information. Anything beyond that or anything that even has a hint of emotion cannot be effectively communicated technologically. This includes anything that's going to make people great. Do you know how to make people great? You look them in the eye. You're going to have some fun conversations that involve back and forth rather than just one-way like in an e-mail. You're going to tell them how much you care about them, you're going tell them how much you appreciate them, and you're going to say, "Thank you" a lot. But you're also sometimes going to say, "We have to talk. There are some things that need to change, and they need to change right away." Let's face it: If you don't do that, how are your people

going to get better?

The truth is that many people set rules
to keep from making decisions.
-- Mike Krzyzewski

Coaching Moments

Blanchard uses a term called the "redirected response" which involves seizing the opportunity when somebody has an attitude or a behavior that's unacceptable—just like a coach. In 2005, I attended a leadership conference by Coach Mike Krzyzewski (known as "Coach K") at Duke University. There were people from all over the world doing workshops and seminars there, and one of the highlights was sitting in on an entire practice with Coach K and his Duke University basketball team. He set them doing their drills, and every 10 or 15 minutes, he would blow the whistle and pull a player aside. He would simply tell the player what he had done wrong and what he needed to do better. Since he did this every 10 or 15 minutes, the players never asked, "Coach, why did you stop practice?" or "Coach, why are you picking on me?" They understood that this was his job.

So, if you never have these important conversations with your people, and these conversations only come out of the blue once in awhile, your people will say, "What'd I do?" and become very distressed. If, on the other hand, you seize your coaching moments every time it makes sense, pulling someone aside to say, "Let's talk about that," your people will come to expect it as just part of what you do to make them better.

Of course, you need to always have these coaching moments privately and one-on-one. Great coaches focus on the person who is in front of them and make that person better. Why? Because you can only make people better one person at a time. You can give great speeches to many, but if you want to make people better, it's a one-on-one experience. I believe that with all my heart.

So, praise your people in front of God and everybody, but the coaching moments need to be one-on-one and a part of your daily routine. That's what great coaches do.

Human behavior is affected by consequences. In animal experiments, the mouse or whatever animal it is in the experiment eventually figures out which button to push in order to get the food pellet. "If I do this action, this is the result." Your job is to let people know when they're doing it right and when they need to do it differently.

Don't store up the frustration and use your anger to drum up the courage for the conversation. Use your coaching moments long before you reach that anger stage, which can be very destructive. Don't allow yourself to be too fearful, too busy, or too distracted.

If you ignore the situation and allow things to escalate, you might end up with your boss determining that there's a problem and criticizing *you* for it. This could even cause you to say, "It isn't me! It's *them!*" But coaches never blame their players. A true coach would say, "I didn't teach them as well as I should, but I'm going to work on that. I wasn't as involved as I should have been, but that's going to change. I will do a better job of coaching." And it's true. If you do a better job of coaching, you will see better performances from your team.

Leadership is a matter of having people look at you
and gain confidence, seeing how you react.
If you're in control, they're in control.

-- Tom Landry

When you're consistent about consequences, and your people come to expect coaching moments, they will actually be disappointed if you let a coaching moment go by. They'll always know where they stand with you, and they will like that. It actually makes them feel safe and secure. It's predictable.

With that being said, coaches are also flexible in dealing with individuals. I have two sons, and they're as different as daylight and dark. This means that the way I deal with them and get the best out of them is different. Stop for a moment right now and think about three or four people on your team and how different they are. Some need praise, while some need a bit of a firm hand to get the best out of them. People are wired differently, and we have to be flexible—especially if we want flexible people on our teams! So, tailor your coaching moments for each individual.

The Players You Want On Your Team

In my seminars, I do an exercise where I ask the participants to tell me about the people they wouldn't want on their team. What qualities are frustrating? One of these might be somebody who wants to sit on the bench. Who wants that? No, you want someone who's going to say, "Put me in, Coach; I'm ready to play." You want people who want to get into the game. You want people who are flexible and can adapt to different circumstances, right? You don't want someone who will get stuck and say, "Well, if it doesn't go this way, I don't know how to do it. I only know what to do if it goes *this* way." Life doesn't work like that, does it? You want people who can take the initiative and have the creativity to figure out how to handle varied situations. You want people who are ready to take on challenges.

If you're a baseball coach, you want somebody who will get up and swing the bat, right? If you're coaching football, you want someone who says, "Give me the ball or throw me the ball. I want the ball; I want to be involved."

Someone who wants to stay on the bench isn't committed to the team or to you as a leader. But what creates this kind of non-committal behavior? More often than not, it's a lack of confidence. "I'm on the bench because I don't believe I know how to do this right." Many times, the job of a coach is to show a player what taking a little risk looks like. The job of a coach is to build up the player and show that person what they're capable of accomplishing.

What other qualities are frustrating in a team member? Perhaps it's someone who has a sense of entitlement. This can be difficult to deal with, can't it? What you want are people who realize they have to earn trust, respect, and rewards. Many businesses have been built around seniority, and seniority can be a good thing or it can be a negative thing. People may feel, "It's my turn" for a promotion even though they may not be best suited for the position. You don't want people who feel entitled. You want people who are going to work hard and earn it whether they're young and inexperienced or mature and experienced.

Before you can win, you have to believe you are worthy.
-- Mike Ditka

This is one of the most important points I'll make: The coach brings his or her values, his or her priorities, and his or her expectations to the team. You may not always win, and your score may not always be the best or the highest. But if you're really dedicated to being a coach and dedicated to your people, the results will get better.

Think about this: It's the people or the program that brings about excellence in terms of the outcome, right? And who controls both? You do. The people on your team are there because you picked them, and you're the one who gets to decide whether you want them there or not. If you don't like it because they're non-committal or entitled, do something about it because chances are, they're not even aware of these issues.

I'm a firm believer that many of these coaching moments that I'm challenging you to have are those daily kinds of interactions that can be matter-of-fact discussions. There's a good chance that your team member will say, "Really? I'm perceived as being entitled? Well, I've got to think about that one. Okay, I'll work on that. Will you help me?"

I believe that much of our behavior is a by-product of how we were raised. So, if one of our parents was a bench-sitter, we'll learn that behavior at such a young age that we won't even be aware that we've carried the behavior into adulthood. It's just normal behavior in the family. We don't even think about it until someone from outside the family points it out. Of course, sometimes, we're insightful enough to figure it out on our own, or we do something that has a really bad outcome. Then, we reflect and realize, "She may be right; I didn't handle that well." But all of us have blind spots and need a teacher at times. We need a teacher to sit us down for a coaching moment and say, "I don't know if you know this about yourself, but..."

Whether your team members exhibit positive or negative behavior, the truth is this: If you want to get rid of the bad and develop more of the good, it's your responsibility. When somebody has a bad attitude that keeps discouraging your team, you must deal with it. Because if you don't, who will?

Your job is to teach every day: "Let's talk about that attitude. You know that I care about you and that I'm here to make you better, right? You remember the first day you came on board? I told you what my job was. My job is to make you better, so we have to have these conversations in order to accomplish that." And if they don't fully understand, just say, "Don't worry. The next time it happens, we'll talk about it again, and eventually, it will be clear to you." Depending on the issue, you might have to have a disciplinary process, but remember that most of these coaching moments don't have to be a big deal. You're not criticizing; you're teaching. It's not just about making it right; it's about helping them to do the best they can.

Some people on your team, of course, will be stars, and some people will do pretty well. Others will just do okay. But your job is to take them as far as they will let you take them. Some people want to grow and get better, and some don't. Some just want a paycheck. I do believe that most people want to become great, but there are those who will refuse to go further. That's just the way it is.

Delivering the Bad News

Years ago, I became an ordained minister and pastored a church in Georgetown, Kentucky when I was in my young twenties. Late one night, I got a phone call, and the person on the other end said, "Is this the Michael Duke who preaches? We're from a church in Red Oak, Alabama." The person went on to say that they needed my help. When someone calls you late at night to ask for your help, it makes you pretty curious, right? Don't forget, I was young—maybe just 23. I was certainly not very seasoned or experienced. So, the guy said, "Well, this is why I have called you. One of our members is a truck driver, and he's at a hotel there in Georgetown, Kentucky. He has been calling all day long to check on his daughter. He's very concerned that she's taken her life, and in fact, she has. What we're worried is going to happen is that he's going to find out that she's dead, and he's going to turn around and barrel back here to Alabama in his rig and hurt himself. We have people on their way to Georgetown right now, but here's what we want you to

46

do. We want you to go to the hotel and tell this gentleman that his daughter is dead, and we want you to stay with him until the people get there from his hometown. Will you do that?"

Now, what do you say to a request like that? How do you say "no" to that? Of course, I said "yes" before I really knew what I was saying. Then, they gave me the clincher: "By the way, he's armed. We want to make sure you know he's armed."

So, I called the state trooper, and he said, "Well, I'll go over there with you." By now, it was after midnight. So I asked the trooper to stay there just long enough to know that everything was okay. So, what happened? Well, the trooper went with me to the motel office, and they gave us the room number of the man from Alabama. The trooper knocked on the motel room door. When the door opened he verified the man's identity and then he said, "This gentleman has something to tell you" and stepped back.

There I was. What do I say? How do I say it? How do you give someone such horrible news? Well, the last thing to do is hem and haw. Have you ever been in a conversation with your boss when he or she just couldn't seem to get to the point? There's bad news to be conveyed, and they just beat around the bush. Well, I learned the lesson at 23 that there's only one way to give bad news, and that is straight up. It's disrespectful, painful, and simply lacking in common courtesy to talk around the harsh truth.

Of course, talking to someone about their performance isn't as dramatic as telling someone about a death, but it's still a very uncomfortable conversation. Again, if your role as a coach is to make people better, you have to have the conversation that makes them better.

So, here's how I told that poor man about his daughter. I said, "Sir, I've got some terrible news. Your friends from Alabama have called me, and they know that you're concerned about your daughter. In fact, she has passed away. She has taken her own life today. They have asked me to come and sit with you until they get here. Will you let me do that?" So, I sat with him until his friends got there, and he drank and cried while we waited. We were in his hotel room, and his suitcase was open with the holstered revolver sitting there in plain sight. I've never seen or heard from this man again. But I learned that day that plain talk, straight up, is the only way to give bad news.

You simply say, "I need to talk to you about your performance. It's less than satisfactory." Or you say, "We have to talk about your attitude. You have missed this expectation, and here's the immediate consequence and ultimate consequence." Be clear about what was unacceptable so that they know how to get better. Don't leave them guessing. Describe it so that they understand how to improve and exactly what the consequences of continuing the behavior will be. Perhaps the ultimate consequence of continuing the behavior will be losing their job. If so, they need to know that. You can say, "I have to have a conversation with you, and I'm not going to enjoy it. But we have to have it anyhow, because unless you get this, you're not going to be the best that you can be."

Many times, as coaches, we're not man or woman enough to tell our team members what they need to do to keep their jobs. Then, when they're terminated, they're surprised. No one should ever be surprised to be fired. It's your job to let any team member know the seriousness of their behavior or attitude problem. In coaching moments, clearly state what they did wrong, how they missed the mark, what the consequence is, and how you're going to help them get better. It's relational, but it's clear in terms of the expectations.

In my seminars, we do role-playing to create hypothetical but common coaching moment scenarios. What follows are four examples of these role-plays.

Scenario #1 – Gossip

In this situation, the problem is gossip. Everyone loves gossip, so this kind of situation happens frequently in the work place. The employee in question works for a hospital and has been with the company for 15 years—long enough to know better than to gossip. This person is talking negatively about other employees, and the leader has to deal with the problem.

Leader: Paul, I want to talk to you about something.

Paul: Okay.

Leader: Well, I've noticed in the unit that there have been some discussions about people regarding their personal lives or things that don't really pertain to work.

Paul: Really? What did you hear?

Leader: What I'm hearing from three different people is that you're talking about others, and some are calling it gossip. I think it's detrimental to the health of the unit and for the company as a whole, so I would prefer that you keep comments that don't pertain to work or that could be considered gossip to yourself and away from the work place.

Paul: Could you be more specific?

Leader: Well, when you're in the break room, and you're complaining about other people or discussing their personal lives, it's inappropriate. We want to watch out for that kind of thing within the work place. If you fail to stop doing this, I'll have to write you up the next time I hear about it, and then, we'll have to continue along the progressive disciplinary path.

It would be common for an employee to ask for clarification about what constitutes gossip, wouldn't it? Gossip is a big, broad thing, and it can be big or small depending upon how damaging the information might be. So, again, clarity is very important. Name it and call it out. If you have to give a specific example, do it. It might hurt feelings, but you need to call the truth as you know it. If the employee says, "Well that's not true," you might need to bring someone else to the conversation and discuss it.

If you have people talking about each other, the best way to fix it is to get them both in your office at the same time. It will stop immediately because it's no longer under wraps. It's all out in the open. You say, "The three of us are going to sit down and have a little meeting. I'm going to nip this in the bud right now."

Scenario #2 – Rudeness

In this next scenario, the problem is rude behavior. This is an employee who has been with the company for 20 years and is consistently rude to people on the telephone. Rather than saying hello, this person answers the phone with, "What do you want?" The leader has already had two conversations with this employee about the rude behavior. A number of people have complained to the leader about the behavior.

Leader: Pam, I need to talk to you. I've had several complaints from customers and coworkers about your speaking to them in a harsh tone. They say that you make curt remarks when you're asked a question and answer the telephone in a rude way.

Pam: Well, I've been here for 20 years, a lot longer than you, and if you look back at my performance history, I've always had good reviews. I really don't think that I have a problem with rudeness.

Leader: Pam, you're right that you do have a great work record and have been here a long time. In that time, you've become accustomed to this behavior, but when you speak to customers and coworkers in a harsh tone, it not only decreases our customer satisfaction, but employee morale goes down, too. I need you to be more cognizant of your tone and the words that you say. Are you willing?

Pam: Yes, I'm willing.

Leader: I also need to remind you that this isn't the first time I've talked to you about this. This is the third time. There will be disciplinary action if we have to have this conversation again.

Pam: All right. I'll do my best.

Leader: Thank you, Pam.

Of course, this is a hypothetical scenario. In the real world, that would be a tough conversation to have, wouldn't it? But you can see in the script that the leader did not flinch and was very clear without being rude or mean. The leader specified to the team member how the behavior affects the rest of the team, as well as the company's reputation with customers. This helps the employee to understand that the behavior has far-reaching effects. The conversation became especially powerful when the leader brought up consequences. Yet, it was a relatively simple conversation. Of course, I know that it doesn't always go so quickly in the real world, but if you, as a leader, remain unflinching, stay clear about your expectations, and specifically state the consequences, you *will* get results nine times out of ten.

Once your employees understand the consequences, it becomes an expectation. In the film *Remember the Titans* that I mentioned earlier, the players come to expect that they'll have to run a mile if they drop the ball. It gets to the point where they don't even wait for the coach to ask them to run. They simply begin running.

So as a leader, you make it clear: "Do you want to work on my team? You can't do it with this behavior. You can't do it with this attitude. It's unacceptable, and here's what will happen if you do it again." If all you do is have the conversation and let it go without the consequence, you've essentially wasted your time. You must actually do what you say you will do in terms of the consequences.

In the sports world, of course, the coach might pull somebody out of the game. A player may even argue that his way to run a play is better than the coach's way. In that case, the coach has to stick to his guns: "As long as I'm the coach, you're going to do it my way." Does that sound harsh? No, it's a coaching moment.

As a leader, if you don't bring the person's attention to the problem, it eventually becomes much bigger. Before you know it, everyone knows about it and wonders when you're going to take care of it. After all, as the leader, it's your job to talk to the employee and fix it. Then, it becomes much more than a coaching moment. It becomes a crucial conversation times ten, and it comes out of nowhere to the employee. You might hear, "Yeah, we've had conversations about it, but you didn't tell me how big a deal it was. It's scary now, and I don't get it. Why didn't you let me know months ago how serious it was?" The bottom line is that it's your job to let folks know not only what the problem is, but how serious it is.

Scenario #3 – Missing Deadlines

In this next scenario, the employee has been missing deadlines. He has been with the company just 18 months, and he has a good attitude. But in the last 60 days or so, he has been missing some deadlines. The team leader has avoided the all-important coaching moments and hasn't yet discussed this problem with him. Now, it has escalated into something big.

Leader: Patrick, I'm glad you came by to see me. You've been a good employee for a good while now, but there's a situation that I need to talk with you about.

Patrick: Oh yeah? What's up?

Leader: Lately, you have missed a few deadlines, and I need for you to know that it's a serious thing. If you start to fall behind, I need you to let me know.

Patrick: It's not always my fault.

Leader: I understand, and I want to hear what we can do to help you meet the deadlines. But first, I want you to know that because of the seriousness of this, it will have some ramifications when your performance review comes up if we can't resolve it.

Patrick: Didn't you just say that I have been a very good employee?

Leader: Yes, you have, but missing deadlines is very serious for the company, and if it continues, it could actually lead to dismissal.

Patrick: Oh, my goodness. So, you're telling me now that if I don't get these reports done on time, you're going to can me?

Leader: That's what I'm telling you.

Patrick: So, am I going to have the resources that I need to get these reports done?

Leader: Yes.

Patrick: Am I going to have a PC that's working all the time, and is the network always going to be up?

Leader: If you find that you don't have the resources that you need, come to me, and I'll make sure you get what you need.

Patrick: That's straightforward enough.

The leader was very clear: "You've missed some deadlines, and if you keep missing deadlines, you can't work here anymore." The light bulb went off for the employee, and there was no question of the consequences. But if somebody on your team is missing deadlines, whose fault is it really? It's your fault, because you haven't made it clear to him or to her that meeting deadlines is critical.

There's a story about a guy named George, who worked for a company that rolled out a new 401K. Everyone had to sign a form about the new 401K, but George was an IT big shot who was busy and didn't want the coverage. So, he didn't sign the form. Eventually, the team leader's boss's boss wanted to know why all of the forms had been turned in except one. The big boss called George into his office and said, "You don't have to take the coverage, but you have to sign the form. If you don't sign it, I'll have to let you go." George took the form immediately and signed it.

The team leader asked George, "Why did you finally sign the form? I've been waiting for you to sign it for months." What do you think George said? "Nobody made it quite as clear to me as you just did that I had to sign it."

So, whose job is it to make things clear to your team? If you complain about your people, shame on you. What are you doing to make things better? What are you doing to make *them* better? What are you doing to stop the undesirable behavior and get them to exhibit better behavior?

Scenario #4 – Sexual Harassment

Next is a very difficult scenario: sexual harassment. The employee has been with the company for eight years. The situation has been discussed to some degree, but now, there has been a major complaint about this employee's behavior. It has come almost to the point of termination.

Leader: Tom, we have to have a conversation again about this situation. What I want to start with is: Do you understand exactly what constitutes sexual harassment? Do you understand the term and how it is defined within the company policy?

Tom: Uh, no.

Leader: Sexual harassment is unsolicited, unwarranted, and unappreciated advances from one person in the work place toward another. It's threatening and unacceptable behavior. We have spoken about it before, but you haven't corrected the behavior. Now, it has progressed to a major situation that is very serious. If it happens again, I won't be able to take action any further at my level. It will go on to HR and possibly end in your termination. Do you understand this?

Tom: I do. Who said that I did this?

Leader: Well, I think you know the answer to that. This is something that we've discussed before, have we not?

Tom: No, not that I remember.

Leader: Yes, we have indeed discussed it. This was unsolicited and uninvited sexually oriented behavior on your part. Do you fully understand that we can't be involved in this kind of practice again?

Tom: Yes, sir.

Leader: Do you understand that one more incident will end in termination for you?

Tom: Yes.

Leader: Very good. I trust we won't have to have this conversation again, then.

It can be difficult to keep your emotions in check when the circumstances are as serious as this, but whatever you do, keep the conversation calm. If you become angry or over-excited, the other person will match your emotion. If you remain calm, there's a much better chance that the employee will also remain calm. You do, of course, have to let the employee know just how big a deal the situation is.

Note that in this scenario, the leader maintained confidentiality and didn't bring up the name of the accusing employee. And even in this situation, the leader treated the employee with respect. He could have lost his cool and said, "You're an idiot," but that would have gotten him nowhere. There is never an excuse to be disrespectful, regardless of the situation. Coaches have to earn the right to speak. When you have values and priorities, and you live those values and priorities, people listen. When you lose your cool and your behavior is out of alignment with your stated values and priorities, people stop listening.

The frequency and quality of your coaching moments determine how you will or won't build a great team. So, even if you have great coaching moments, but you don't have them often, those moments will be ineffective. When you have quality coaching moments *often*, you will transform the people who work on your team. There's no way to avoid transforming them because that's what great coaches do. That's what Lombardi did with the Packers; that's what coach Wooden did with UCLA; that's what Pat Summitt did with the Lady Vols. They took their program and their values, and they transformed the individuals on their teams. The challenge as a leader is to take your role seriously and to care enough to deliver the bad news. If someone is late, you simply say straight up: "I want to have a conversation with you because you're late all the time, and if you continue to be late, you will be terminated." What other way is there to say it?

Whether it's a bad attitude or sexual harassment, a coach calls the person out because the coach knows that if the players don't know what they're doing wrong, they can't do anything differently. They can't learn to be better.

I know it's difficult. You may find yourself leading people who are considerably older than you. I was a sales manager at age 26, and I had a team of 15 people, every one of them older than me. But coaches can work with everyone regardless of where they are and make them better. They can do this because they understand that regardless of whether we're 26 or 66, we all have more to learn. You have something to teach me, and I have something to teach you. So, a coach doesn't approach his team as if he knows it all. We're all learners. There is no point when you get there and say, "I've got it! I'm a leader now, and I can teach other people about leadership." Leaders continue to learn and grow, and they understand that everyone is somewhere in this leadership continuum. And the leader's job is to move everyone a little bit further on the way. When we know that we're all continuously learning and growing, we're gracious toward others when they make a mistake.

If you think everyone should do things right the first time, every little mistake becomes a big deal. "How could you drop that pass?" "How could you miss that play?" The fact is that I still make mistakes, and I'm going to drop the pass. But that's not going to change the fact that it's going to be reviewed so that I can practice and improve. Coaches understand that they're teachers and that everyone on their team is a learner, especially themselves.

Make sure that team members know
they are working with you, not for you.

-- John Wooden

The Power of Celebration

Besides these private coaching moments where you have to call someone out for behavior or for not meeting expectations, you also need to be encouraging. As I said before, the coaching moments are private and one-on-one, but when you praise your team members, do it in front of others!

Let's face it: People have all sorts of problems going on in their lives at any given time. Someone may be dealing with an ill child or parent. Someone else may just be having a hard time mastering a skill. First and foremost, they need to know that you believe in them. Again, many of these folks have never had anyone believe in them. No one has ever said to them, "Good job."

I'm lucky because I was blessed with parents who told me from day one that I could do anything that I put my mind to. But many people never got that kind of encouragement, and you need to make sure that they hear it from you.

You can't live a perfect day without doing something for someone who will never be able to repay you.

-- John Wooden

The truth is simple: if you don't believe in them, they shouldn't be on your team. If you don't believe in them, they'll know. And when you stop believing in them, they'll know. You'll stop spending time with them and stop teaching them. You'll work with the people you do believe in, and the ones who are left out will pick up on it.

I have two boys, and we love baseball. One of my greatest joys in life as a father was to go to Little League games and watch my kids play. It's very rare in t-ball for a kid to hit the ball very far, of course. They're just learning the game. But one beautiful summer day about 15 years ago, a player from the opposing team hit the ball hard, and it went right toward my son who was playing on the pitcher's mound. He brought his glove up as much to shield himself from the ball as anything, but the coolest thing happened. He looked at his glove and realized that he had caught the ball! I was sitting right behind home plate, and he looked at me and said, "I caught the ball!" Everyone applauded and came up to him afterward saying, "Great catch,

Alex!" and "Way to go!" He was only about four years old, but he felt like a professional baseball player.

I don't have any recollection of the score or the inning that day. It didn't matter because it was one of the sweetest moments in and of itself. Later, when we talked about it, Alex said, "Dad, can you believe I caught the ball?" I said, "Yeah, Son, that was a great catch!" Truth be told, I don't know how much was skill and how much was just reaction. But what if I had said, "That was a lucky catch, Son. Don't make too big a deal out of it." What if I'd said a day or two later, "When are you going to make a catch like that again?"

My point is that there is an important power in celebration. When we think about celebrations, we usually think about parties or big events. Those are certainly great things, but celebrations need to happen every single day. Sometimes, it's just looking at somebody and saying, "Good job. Thank you!" Sometimes, it's just saying, "Hey, everyone, come over here. Gather around. I've never seen this task done better. Way to go." Then, everyone goes back to work. It's a small moment of celebration and appreciation of excellence, but it's important.

There are all sorts of opportunities to celebrate the little extraordinary things that happen—both at work and at home. Don't be discouraging to people who are trying to do great things. As I've said, people want to do great things. They want to be better, so build them up. Praise is absolutely essential. Again, criticize in private, but praise before the whole world.

I believe that there are so many people in this world who have lived way too long without affirmation. They're thirsty for someone to care enough to notice that they bent over backwards to do a good job. So, when they do something genuinely praiseworthy, it means the world to them to be appreciated.

Imagine this scenario: You're at a Little League game, and you're coaching six-year olds. Your job is just to teach them the basics. "Here's how you hold the bat, and here's how you swing." They'll set their eyes, and when the ball comes in, they'll swing and miss it by three feet. But you say, "Way to go! Way to swing the bat!" One day, a kid will swing and nick the ball. The kid will be excited and say, "I got a foul tip! Can you believe it?" As the coach, you'll say, "Hey! Way to go! You almost hit it!" Then comes the day when the kid will hit the ball and will run straight to third instead of first base. And as the coach, you won't react angrily and scream, "No, you're supposed to run to first!" Instead you yell, "Great hit!" You celebrate the hit and talk about running to first base later.

With your people, make it first about the hit. Then, talk to them about running to first base. You have choices with your people every day. You can either build them up or run them down. A coach who praises his players and continues to instruct them is a coach whose instruction the players will heed.

One of the things you need to say is: "Here's what I expect. If you'll be on my team, you'll grow. If you'll be on my team, I'll commit to you and will help you get better. If you strive to meet this expectation, you will be great one day." Just like that, the little boy who missed the ball, then foul-tipped it, then hit it and ran to the wrong base, will figure it out and become a great hitter. Do you think he wanted to give up when he was missing the ball? He didn't say, "I'm not a good baseball player, Coach. Just put me on the bench. I don't want to play anymore." No, the kid kept trying and finally said, "Coach, you were right! I can hit the ball now!"

I've seen leaders, owners, and executives struggle with saying nice things to people. I've heard them say, "I don't need praise. Nobody ever praised me." But it just doesn't make any sense because we are all thirsty for praise.

Start Easy

If you've ever been to Sea World, you've probably been to the show with Shamu or one of Shamu's cousins—the killer whales. If you sit in the front row, the killer whale jumps over a stick that might be as high as 20 feet in the air.

Ken Blanchard wrote a book called *Whale Done,* which chronicled his work with a whale trainer to learn how to use these principles with people. So, how do you train a killer whale? Well, first you find out what a killer whale likes. What kind of fish is its favorite? Then, you put the stick on the bottom of the pool, and when the whale swims over to the stick, it gets a treat of its favorite fish. You don't test the whale very much in the beginning. You slowly build up to that high jump. The expectation of the whale by the trainer increases incrementally with a treat offered after each success or near success.

It's the same with your people. When they're new, you want to make it easy. You don't want to frustrate them or give them too high a goal at first. You want to put the stick at the bottom of the pool. Then, raise it up a foot until you build up gradually to the big jump. When you get to the jump, it will be a "Wow!" moment. You may have been working on it for a while, but it will be worth it. You will start with the stick at the bottom, and you will gradually praise them as they make each slight incremental improvement. Then, before you know it, it will become a "Wow!" moment.

Now, I don't know what happens if you criticize a killer whale, but what do you think happens if you quit feeding him his treat? You might say to the whale, "You know what I'm expecting. Go to the stick. I shouldn't have to give you the treat every time." Of course, that attitude contradicts the whole idea of consequence, and it confuses the whale.

Consequences have to be consistent, and praise is a powerfully motivating consequence. When you praise people part of the time and become distracted or detached at other times, they become confused. They might think, "It was important the other day, but I did the same thing even better today. I guess it isn't so important after all. Do they want me to do it or not?" You have to be consistent in order to continue getting the best from your people.

If you make every game a life and death proposition, you're going to have problems. For one thing, you'll be dead a lot.

-- Dean Smith

You Invited Them

I have a client who is a legend in his industry, and he asked me to work with a group of his leaders. One of the first questions I like to ask of new leaders is: "When is the last time anyone was terminated?" This particular group looked at each other and smiled awkwardly. I said, "Why is that question so funny?" Their answer was, "Well, we don't terminate people."

My next question, of course, was, "What do you do when somebody doesn't do their job properly?" They said, "Well, the president just stops returning their calls." The president of the company just ignores the people who are not performing well. He thinks they'll just "go away." The great people, of course, move on to a place where they're respected, but the mediocre or poor people just stay there.

So, the people on your team are there because you've invited them to be there. You choose every day to keep them on your team. Do they belong there? If you find yourself complaining about them every day and there's nothing genuinely praiseworthy about their behavior, maybe it's time to trade up. Of course, again, you must have a disciplinary process that you go through. But use that process. Don't whine and complain about your people. Coaches never do that. They take responsibility for their people because they know that they are responsible for picking the players on their team.

A Coach's Commitment

In order to build a great team that gives you consistently great performances, you have to be a coach every single day and commit to making your people the best they can be. That's how you sustain great performance over the long-term. If you invest yourself 110% in your people, the numbers will come. You will be able to quantify the performance. Do you believe that?

The bottom line is that if you seize the coaching moments frequently and consistently, your people will get better little by little every single day. And one day, you'll arrive at a "Wow!" moment.

Last year, there was a very small softball game in the Division II Women's Fast-Pitch Softball league. Western Oregon was playing Central Washington, and Western Oregon had won the day before 8-1. On this particular day, it was the second inning, and no one had scored yet. Sarah Tucholsky of Western Oregon came up to bat. She was a 5'2" part-time player who was a senior and had never hit a home run in her life. She always gave it her best, was very well-liked and a great team player, but she had never hit a home run. There were two players on base, and Sarah hit the second pitch with a hard WHAP! Sarah didn't realize that she had hit a home run until everyone started cheering. So, she rounded first and suddenly realized that she had never stepped on first base. As she turned to go back toward first, she twisted her knee and tore some ligaments, falling down on first base in a heap. The other two players on the bases scored, but Sarah couldn't walk.

The coach asked if they could put in a pinch runner. The umpire said, "Yeah, but it's a single with two RBIs if you do." So, the coach said, "What if we help her get across the bases?" But the umpire said, "Then, she's out. You can't touch her until she gets around the bases." So, the coach saw no choice, "We're going to have to put in a pinch runner."

Then, there was a voice from Mallory Holtman, the first baseman for the other team, Central Washington. She said, "What if *we* help her around the bases?" The umpire was dumbfounded and said, "I don't know any rule against that." So, Mallory called over Liz Wallace, the shortstop, and they picked up their opponent, gently taking her to second base. Then, they took her to third base, and she touched third. They took her to home plate, and she touched home. Western Oregon was up 3 to nothing and went on to win the game.

Central Washington may have lost that game, but they weren't losers. They won because they knew what the real goal was. Talk about a "Wow!" moment. Mallory Holtman was interviewed after the game, and she said, "I don't know what the big deal is. I mean, she hit it over the fence. She's a senior." Mallory was the home run batting leader for that conference, and she said she was glad they made a big deal out of it because it let people know what their program stands for, who they are, and what they value. Mallory was coached to the goal. She was taught by her coach what winning is really about, and that's why this was a "Wow!" moment.

Central Washington's coach said, "I'm forever changed. I've never seen anything like it. I'm moved that my players would exhibit such character, would exhibit such integrity and such compassion."

That's the kind of people you want on your team, right? But first, that's the kind of leader that you need to be, teaching your people that the quality of their character, the level of their integrity, and the passion in their hearts is far more important than any score on a board.

Mallory Holtman's behavior that day was no accident. It was not a random event. The choice she made to carry Sara Tucholsky around the bases was a result of the leadership she received in her life. Her parents and her coaches all worked hard to teach and train her to be excellent. That quiet summer day we all got to see the "Wow." We were all reminded what winning really means and what excellence looks like.

You are a leader, a coach. Your team is counting on you to lead in a way that really counts. There are Mallory Holtmans on your team. Help them become the very best they can be. It is never about the win or the loss—never about the numbers. You can lose by the numbers over and over and over again but still be a winner if you lead like a legendary coach.

Acknowledgements

This book would not be possible without the efforts of my son Evan Alex Duke. Alex is a talented writer and blogger in his own right. Because of his energy, talent and expertise in editing, this project was moved off the back burner and became I reality. Alex, thank you! I appreciate your talent and am so proud of you as a writer and most importantly of the man you have become!

Recommended Reading on the Subject of Coaching

1. Coach to the Goal by Michael Duke
2. Everyone's A Coach by Ken Blanchard and Don Shula
3. What It Takes to be #1 by Vince Lombardi Jr
4. America's Coach by Ross Bernstein
5. Wooden on Leadership by John Wooden and Steve Jamison
6. Leading With the Heart by Mike Krzyzewski and Donald Phillips
7. Winning Every Day by Lou Holtz
8. Raise the Roof by Pat Summit
9. Lead to Succeed by Rick Pitino
10. Built to Win by John Schuerholz and Larry Guest

The following list has been compiled to challenge the truly hungry and curious. It is composed of books that have profoundly influenced Michael's thinking and therefore his personal and management philosophy.

Michael's Top 10

1. "The One Minute Manager" by Ken Blanchard and Spencer Johnson

2. "The Seven Habits of Highly Effective People" by Stephen Covey

3. "Love is the Killer App" by Tim Sanders

4. "The Customer Comes Second", by Hal F. Rosenbluth and Diane McFerrin Peters

5. "When Pride Still Mattered, A Life of Vince Lombardi" by David Maraniss

6. "The Leadership Challenge" by James M. Kouzes and Barry Z. Posner

7. "Putting the One Minute Manager to Work" by Ken Blanchard Ph. D. and Robert Lorber M.D.

8. "Whale Done" by Ken Blanchard Ph. D., Thad Lucinak, Chuck Tompkins and Jim Ballard

9. "Primal Leadership" by Daniel Goleman

10. "Good to Great" by Jim Collins

About the Author

Michael Duke has led a remarkably diversified life. He has been in the ministry, sales, corporate management and most recently an entrepreneur. Michael Duke is not only a gifted communicator; he truly understands people, which is why Michael is so successful at getting to the heart of so many issues. It may have been Michael's brief career in the ministry, which has served as an important foundation for his success in motivating and managing people.

Michael began his sales and marketing career 20 years ago with Curtis Industries, a national hardware company, where he ranked in the top 10 of 250 sales associates and was accepted in the prestigious Presidents Inner Circle. At age 26, Michael became the youngest district manager in the country.

He has also enjoyed a distinguished management career with *Auto Trader* magazine in which he orchestrated a successful turnaround and facilitated an acquisition of a primary competitor. While accomplishing this phenomenal success in his career, he earned a graduate degree in Management in 1986.

Michael soon discovered that he had the heart of a teacher and began a parallel career as a college instructor. As a natural outgrowth of his love for teaching and helping others, Michael established his consulting business in 2000 and now devotes his full schedule consulting and speaking to businesses in the region.

Many can personally attest that Michael's passion is people. He is a motivator and problem solver. Some refer to Michael as "Louisville's best business teacher." But his clients simply refer to him as "trusted friend and advisor."

Share It with Others

To order single copies of *Lead Like a Coach,* simply
Call Harrods Creek Publishing at **(502) 648-6260**
Or
Visit Michael Duke online at **www.michaelduke.com**.

Lead Like a Coach and other books by Harrods Creek Publishing are available at special quantity discounts for bulk purchases for sales promotions, premiums, fund- raising or educational use. Special books or book excerpts also can be created to fit individual needs.

For details about bulk quantity purchases and more information, call Harrods Creek Publishing at **(502) 648-6260** or write to:

Harrods Creek Publishing
P.O. Box 43784
Louisville, Kentucky 40253

How to Invite Michael to Speak

If you would like Michael to come and share the 10 truths of the *Coach to the Goal* message with your team, call 502-426-0808 or visit www.michaelduke.com.

Michael consults with organizations and coaches owners and executives based on the philosophy within the pages of Lead Like A Coach. If the message resonates with you he would love to speak with you and discuss how he may bring value to your team.

Lead Like A Coach is also a presentation that can be delivered in formats from one to six hours. You will find Michael to be an engaging speaker. He is passionate about making a positive difference in the lives of the people who matter most to you.

.

www.ingramcontent.com/pod-product-compliance
Lightning Source LLC
Chambersburg PA
CBHW071228170526
45165CB00003B/1042